THE BEST
CATS
EVER

# Persians are the Best!

Elaine Landau

LERNER PUBLICATIONS COMPANY · MINNEAPOLIS

Lerner Publications Company
A division of Lerner Publishing Group, Inc.
241 First Avenue North
Minneapolis, MN 55401 U.S.A.

Website address: www.lernerbooks.com

Library of Congress Cataloging-in-Publication Data

Landau, Elaine.
       Persians are the best! / by Elaine Landau.
          p.    cm. — (The best cats ever)
       Includes index.
       ISBN 978-0-7613-6425-2 (lib. bdg. : alk. paper)
       1. Persian cat.  I. Title.
    SF449.P4L36  2011
    636.8'32—dc22                          2010025282

Manufactured in the United States of America
1 — CG — 12/31/10

# TABLE OF CONTENTS

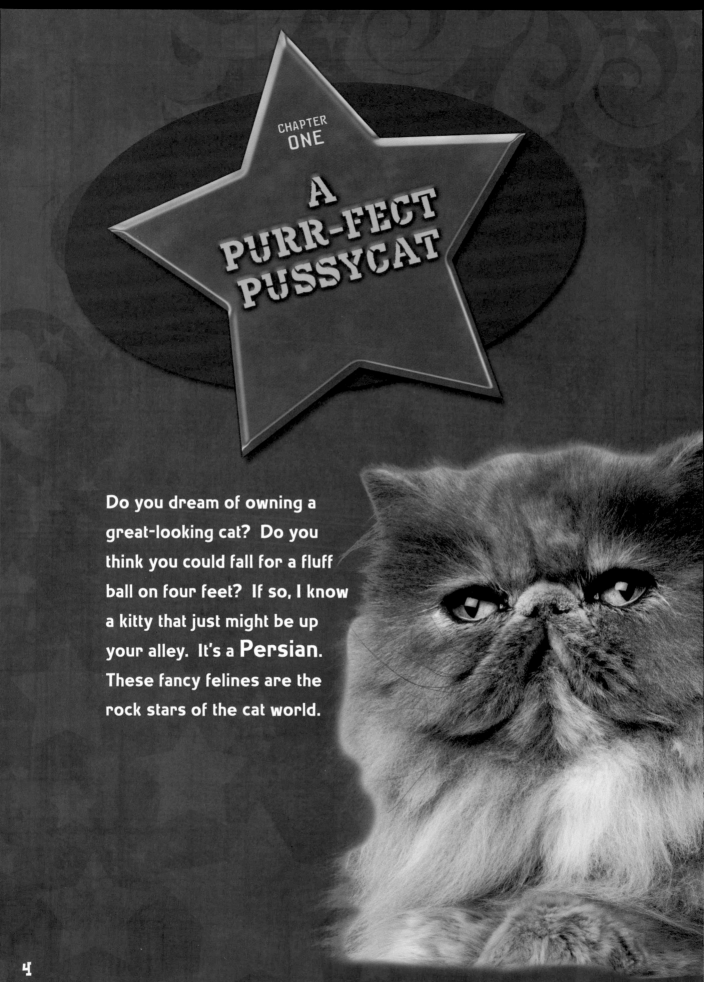

# A PURR-FECT PUSSYCAT

Do you dream of owning a great-looking cat? Do you think you could fall for a fluff ball on four feet? If so, I know a kitty that just might be up your alley. It's a **Persian**. These fancy felines are the rock stars of the cat world.

# Cat Eye Candy

There's a lot to love about a Persian. They have cute, stocky bodies and short, sturdy legs. Their flat baby faces and big eyes can melt your heart.

## THE NAME GAME

A super cat needs a super name. Do any of these fit your pretty Persian?

Jasmine          WOODRUFF          Adonis

                    Omar     Merlin        Sheba

Moonbeam

                            Isis        Princess

Avery

The Persian's crowning glory is its long, flowing coat. These cats also have a thick ring of fur around their necks. It's called a ruff. It makes them look like little lions.

A Persian's ruff gives it a lionlike appearance.

Some Persians are a solid color. They may be white, black, cream, blue (a shade of gray), or another color. Other Persians have coats with patterns. All are beauties!

This is a blue Persian.

This Persian is multicolored.

## ON THE BIG SCREEN

Did you ever see the Disney movie *The Aristocats*? The star of this cartoon is a lovely white Persian named Duchess (far right). Duchess may just be one of the cutest cartoon cats ever drawn.

# A Simply Charming Cat

Persians are not just pretty kitties.
They are friendly and fun too.
Persians love being with
their human families. They
like being picked up and
cuddled. They are
known for being calm,
gentle pets.

# CHECK OUT THOSE PEEPERS!

Eye color in Persian cats varies. White Persians usually have blue- or copper-colored eyes. But some white Persians have an unusual eye color. They have one copper eye and one blue eye. These cats are known as odd-eyed Persians.

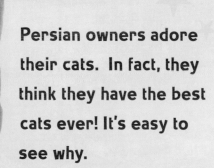

Persian owners adore their cats. In fact, they think they have the best cats ever! It's easy to see why.

CHAPTER
TWO

# WAY BACK WHEN

Persian cats come from the Middle East. They got their start in the country of Persia. These days, that country is known as Iran.

This cat sculpture is in Iran's Golestan Palace.

In the 1800s, traders from Europe often went to the Middle East. The area was rich with treasures. Traders could find spices, silks, and jewels there.

The traders found something else in Persia too. It was the beautiful, long-haired Persian cat. They took these cats back with them to Europe.

European traders to the Middle East fell in love with the Persian cat.

# What a Cat!

Persian cats were a hit throughout Europe. No one had ever seen such a fancy cat before. Everyone wanted to own one.

A British artist painted this Persian cat, named Psyche, in 1787.

*Psyche*

## CATS IN ANCIENT HISTORY

The ancient Egyptians worshipped cats. The Egyptian goddess Bast had a woman's body and a cat's head. The Egyptians made it a crime to kill or harm a cat.

A statue of the Egyptian goddess Bast

The 1877 book *Pets of the Family*, featured this illustration of a Persian cat by a British artist.

The first cat show in Britain took place in July 1871. The Persians stole the show. One of the winners was a blue-eyed white Persian. A pretty blue Persian was another showstopper.

## A ROYAL KITTY

Queen Victoria (*right*), Britain's queen from 1837 to 1901, owned two Persians. Louis XV, king of France from 1715 to 1774, had a Persian too. The Persian's glamorous looks made it a popular pet among royals.

# Coming to America

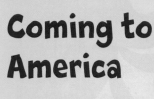

In the late 1800s, Persians were brought to the United States. The first known to arrive was a black Persian from Spain. Next came a white one from Persia. In time, many more were brought over from Europe.

Persians were a hit in the United States too. They often won first prize at cat shows. But families also wanted these appealing cats as pets. Persians soon became the country's most popular cat breed.

Four women prepare their blue Persians for a cat show in 1937.

# PERSIANS MAKE THEIR MARK ON HISTORY

Florence Nightingale *(right)* was a famous British nurse and writer. She is known as the founder of modern nursing. But did you know she was also a cat lover?

Nightingale owned many cats during her lifetime. Among these was a fine family of Persian kitties. A few of these Persians were always getting into things. They'd knock over flower vases and nap on piles of books and reports. Often they'd tip over bottles of ink and step into the ink puddle they created. Their inky paw prints can still be seen on many of Nightingale's writings. You could say that these cats really made their mark on history!

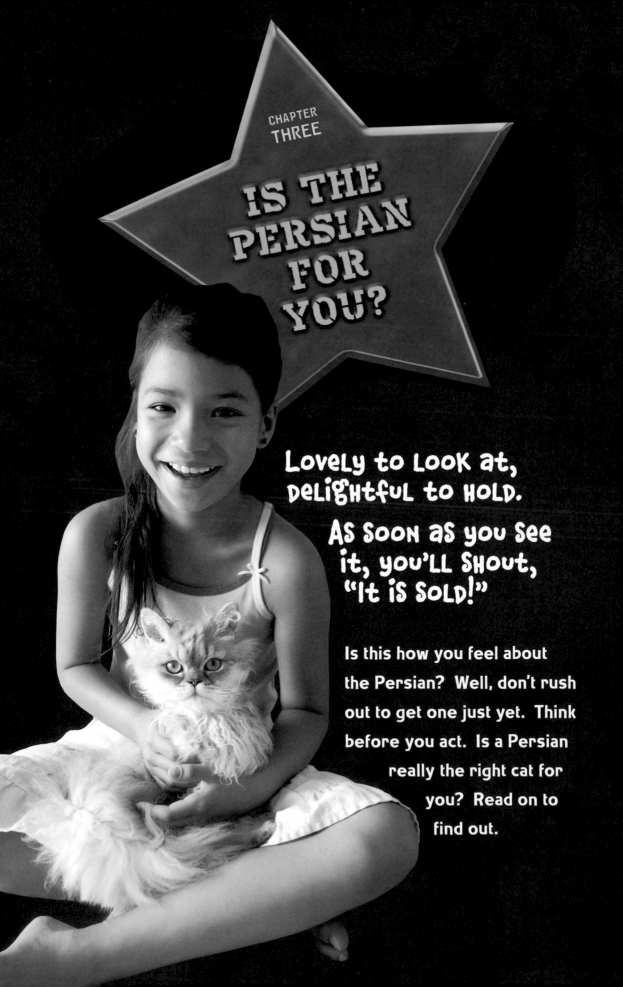

CHAPTER
THREE

# IS THE PERSIAN FOR YOU?

Lovely to look at,
delightful to hold.
As soon as you see
it, you'll shout,
"It is sold!"

Is this how you feel about
the Persian? Well, don't rush
out to get one just yet. Think
before you act. Is a Persian
really the right cat for
you? Read on to
find out.

# Cat Care Needed— Big Time!

Are you looking for an easy-to-care-for cat? If so, don't get a Persian. Persians don't look picture perfect on their own. They must be groomed to look great.

Persian cats should be brushed daily. This keeps their coats from getting matted. You will also need to clean the fur around your Persian's eyes. Persians tend to have watery eyes. The tears can stain their fur if you don't wipe them away.

# Hair Here, There, and Everywhere

Persians shed a lot. There's no getting around it. If you get a Persian, you'll find cat hair on your furniture, clothing, and toys.

Do you have allergies? Can't stand the idea of having cat hair on your things? Then pass on getting a Persian.

Long-haired Persian cats will shed on furniture.

## HANDLE WITH CARE

Do you have younger brothers or sisters? Are they sometimes noisy or rough? Teach them to be gentle with your Persian. They need to know that a cat is a living thing. It can't be treated like a toy.

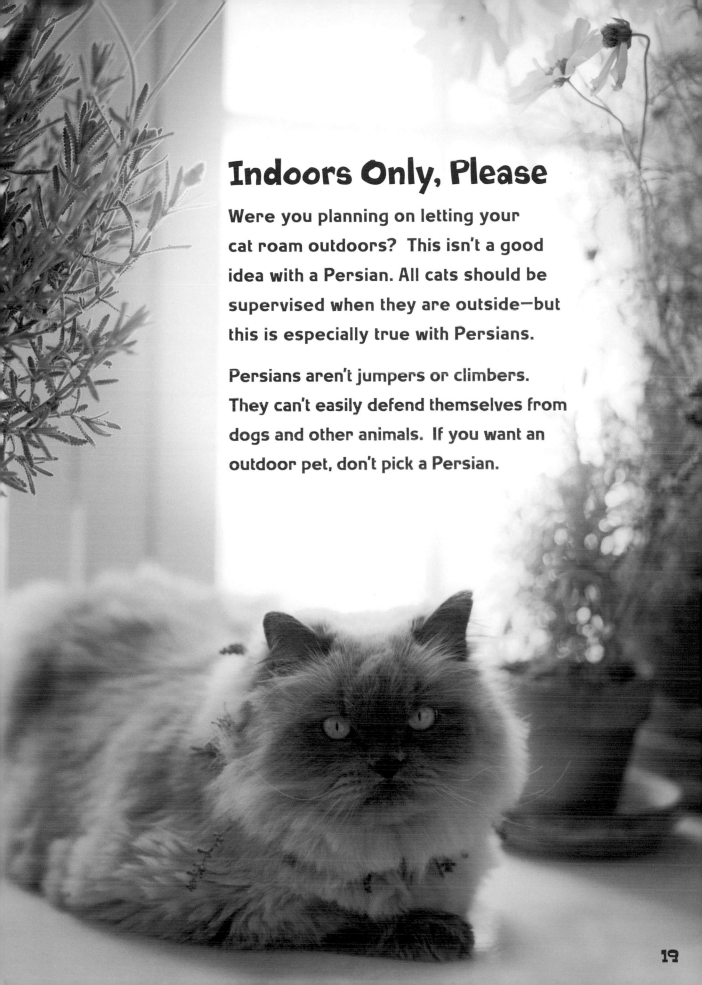

# Indoors Only, Please

Were you planning on letting your cat roam outdoors? This isn't a good idea with a Persian. All cats should be supervised when they are outside—but this is especially true with Persians.

Persians aren't jumpers or climbers. They can't easily defend themselves from dogs and other animals. If you want an outdoor pet, don't pick a Persian.

# Pricey Pussycats

Persians are purebred cats. This means they can be costly. Breeders might charge $650 or more for a Persian kitten.

Persians can be costly in other ways too. Many Persian owners take their cats to professional groomers. This keeps the cat's coat in top shape. But trips to the groomer can add up. Can your family afford them?

Purebred Persian kitties

Groomers often have special shampoos and equipment to make your cat beautiful.

## RESCUE A PERSIAN

Persian kittens are expensive—but how about getting an older cat? Many lovely older Persians can be found at rescue centers for this breed. You can often take one home for a small fee.

Of course, you'll still need to spend money on food, toys, and grooming. But rescuing a Persian *can* help cut down on the purchase price.

Now you know more about the Persian. Do you still think it's the cat for you? If so, you're really lucky. You're about to get a great new family member. Your Persian will be beautiful, friendly, and loving. Get ready to fall for a super pet!

# CHAPTER FOUR

# COMING HOME

It's a great day. You couldn't be more excited. You're going to pick up your Persian pussycat!

# Are You Ready?

You want your new cat to feel at home. So have some basic supplies ready for your furry friend. Here's a list of items to get you started:

- food and water bowls

- cat food

- litter box

- kitty litter

- brush and wide-tooth steel comb

- scratching post

- cat carrier

# It's a Good Bet to See a Vet

Take your cute kitty to a veterinarian right away. That's a doctor who cares for animals. They are called vets for short.

## PLAY WITH YOUR PUSSYCAT

Persians are not highly active cats. But they still like to have fun. You can find cat toys at most pet shops. Try a few. See which your cat likes best.

The vet will make sure your cat is healthy. Your Persian will also get the shots it needs. You'll see your vet again. Be sure to take your cat to the vet for regular checkups. Also take your cat to the vet if it gets sick.

A vet can let you know if your Persian needs shots or medicine.

# Feeding Your Fluff Ball

Ask your vet what to feed your cat. Cats need different foods as they grow older. Stick to cat food. Don't share your birthday cake with kitty. This can lead to an unhealthful weight gain.

## USE TREATS WISELY

Don't give your cat treats for dessert. Use cat treats as rewards for good behavior. Did your cat learn to use its scratching post instead of the couch? Give that cat a treat!

# Get Ready to Groom

Don't forget to brush your Persian daily. Be very gentle
when you do this. Many cats come to love being brushed.

# You and Your Persian

Your Persian will love you all its life. Be an owner your cat can be proud of. Make sure your cat always has fresh food and clean water. Groom and play with your cat every day. Return the love your cat gives you. That's what being a good pet owner is really all about.

# GLOSSARY

**breed:** a particular type of cat. Cats of the same breed have the same body shape and general features.

**breeder:** someone who mates cats to produce a particular kind of cat

**coat:** a cat's fur

**feline:** a cat, or having to do with cats

**groom:** to clean, brush, and trim a cat's coat

**matted:** severely tangled. Matted fur clumps together in large masses.

**purebred:** a cat whose parents are of the same breed

**rescue center:** a shelter where stray and abandoned cats are kept until they are adopted

**ruff:** a thick ring of fur around a cat's neck

**shed:** to lose fur

**veterinarian:** a doctor who treats animals. Veterinarians are called vets for short.

# FOR MORE INFORMATION

## Books

Brecke, Nicole, and Patricia M. Stockland. *Cats You Can Draw*. Minneapolis: Millbrook Press, 2010. Perfect for cat lovers, this colorful book teaches readers how to draw many popular cat breeds, including the Persian.

Britton, Tamara L. *Persian Cats*. Edina, MN: Abdo, 2011. Learn more about the Persian cat in this title.

Brown, Ruth. *Gracie the Lighthouse Cat*. London: Andersen Press, 2011. Gracie the lighthouse cat and Grace Darling, the lighthouse keeper's daughter, both have an adventure one very windy night.

Harris, Trudy. *Tally Cat Keeps Track*. Minneapolis: Millbrook Press, 2011. Tally McNally is a cat who loves to tally—but one day, he gets into a jam. Will his friends find a way to help him?

Landau, Elaine. *Your Pet Cat*. Rev. ed. New York: Children's Press, 2007. This selection is a good guide for young people on choosing and caring for a cat.

Stone, Lynn M. *Persian Cats*. Vero Beach, FL: Rourke Publishing, 2010. Stone describes the Persian cat's personality and provides an interesting history of the breed.

## Websites

### ASPCA Kids

http://www.aspca.org/aspcakids

Check out this website for helpful hints on caring for a cat and other pets.

### For Kids: About Cats

http://kids.cfa.org

Be sure to visit this website about cats and cat shows. Don't miss the link to some fun games as well.

LERNER & SOURCE™

Expand learning beyond the printed book. Download free, complementary educational resources for this book from our website, www.lernerresource.com.

# Index

# Photo Acknowledgments

The images in this book are used with the permission of: backgrounds © iStockphoto.com/javarman3 and © iStockphoto.com/Julie Fisher; © iStockphoto.com/Michael Balderas, p. 1; © Eric Isselée/ Dreamstime.com, pp. 4-5, 11 (top); © NaturePL/SuperStock, p. 5; © Arco Images GmbH/Alamy, pp. 6-7 (both); © Dorling Kindersley/Getty Images, p. 7 (top inset); © Walt Disney Pictures/courtesy Everett Collection, p. 7 (bottom inset); © iStockphoto.com/ronen, p. 8; © iStockphoto.com/Kati Neudert, p. 9 (top); © Robert Estall photo agency/Alamy, p. 9 (bottom); © Idealink Photography/Alamy, p. 10; © iStockphoto. com/Suzanne Mulligan, p. 11 (bottom); National Trust Photographic Library/Derrick E. Witty/The Bridgeman Art Library, p. 12 (main); © Ivy Close Images/Alamy, p. 12 (inset); © Mary Evans Picture Library/ The Image Works, p. 13 (top); © Christie's Images Ltd./SuperStock, p. 13 (bottom); © Dave King/Dorling Kindersley/Getty Images, pp. 14, 21 (bottom), 28; © Fred Morley/Fox Photos/Hulton Archive/Getty Images, pp. 14-15; © Hulton Archive/Getty Images, p. 15; © Lisa B./CORBIS, p. 16; © Fiona Green, pp. 17, 21 (top); © SuperStock/SuperStock, p. 18 (top); © GK Hart/Vikki Hart/Stone/Getty Images, p. 18 (bottom); © Amy Neunsinger/Stone/Getty Images, p. 19; © Juniors Bildarchiv/Photolibrary, pp. 20 (top), 20-21; © Simon Marcus/CORBIS, p. 22; © Aflo/naturepl.com, p. 23; © Agita Leimane/Dreamstime.com, p. 24 (left); © Mark Bond/Dreamstime.com, p. 24 (right top); © Eti Swinford/Dreamstime.com, p. 24 (right center); © iStockphoto.com/Jennifer Sheets, p. 24 (right bottom); © iStockphoto.com/Mehmet Salih Guler, p. 25 (top); © Eyewave/Dreamstime.com, p. 25 (bottom); © VStock/Alamy, p. 26 (top); © Southern Stock Corp/CORBIS, p. 26 (bottom); © iStockphoto.com/Isabelle Mory, p. 27 (top); © Petra Wegner/ naturepl.com, p. 27 (bottom); © Steve Gorton and Tim Ridley/Dorling Kindersley/Getty Images, p. 29 (left); © Grapheast/Alamy, p. 29 (right).

Front cover: © Photodisc/Getty Images.
Back cover: © Eric Isselée/Dreamstime.com.